Cindy Bentley

D1373352

Other Badger Biographies

Belle and Bob La Follette: Partners in Politics
Caroline Quarlls and the Underground Railroad
Casper Jaggi: Master Swiss Cheese Maker
Curly Lambeau: Building the Green Bay Packers
Dr. Kate: Angel on Snowshoes
Frank Lloyd Wright and His New American Architecture
Gaylord Nelson: Champion for Our Earth
Harley and the Davidsons: Motorcycle Legends
Mai Ya's Long Journey
Mountain Wolf Woman: A Ho-Chunk Girlhood
Ole Evinrude and His Outboard Motor
A Recipe for Success: Lizzie Kander and Her Cookbook
Richard Bong: World War II Flying Ace
Tents, Tigers, and the Ringling Brothers

Cindy Bentley

Spirit of a Champion

Bob Kann and Caroline Hoffman

Wisconsin Historical Society Press

Published by the Wisconsin Historical Society Press
Publishers since 1855

wisconsin**history**.org

This publication was funded, in part, by the Wisconsin Board for People with Developmental Disabilities. Federal funds were provided under PL 106-402 through a grant authorized by the Administration on Developmental Disabilities and the U.S. Department of Health and Human Services. Board grantees are encouraged to freely express their findings and conclusions. These points of view do not necessarily represent the official position of the Wisconsin Board for People with Developmental Disabilities.

Front cover image courtesy of Special Olympics Wisconsin

Printed in the United States of America
Designed by Jill Bremigan

14 13 12 11 10   1 2 3 4 5

Library of Congress Cataloging-in-Publication Data

Kann, Bob.
   Cindy Bentley : spirit of a champion / Bob Kann and Caroline Hoffman.
      p. cm.—(Badger biographies)
   Includes bibliographical references and index.
   ISBN 978-0-87020-456-2 (pbk. : alk. paper) 1. Bentley, Cindy. 2. Athletes—Wisconsin—Biography. 3. Special Olympics—Biography. 4. Developmentally disabled children—Wisconsin—Biography. 5. Developmental disabilities—Biography. I. Hoffman, Caroline. II. Title.
   GV697.B44K36 2010
   796.092—dc22
   [B]

2010001910

This book is dedicated to Cindy Bentley. Your great spirit is an inspiration to us all.

Publication of this book was made possible, in part, by a gift from the Wisconsin Board for People with Developmental Disabilities.

Contents

1

Meet Cindy Bentley

Cindy Bentley did not grow up living in a home with her parents. Instead, she spent most of her childhood in an **institution**. There, she and other children with disabilities were cared for by grown-ups who worked for the State of Wisconsin. At the institution, Cindy had few opportunities to meet new people, go to new places, and try new things. This made Cindy feel as though she lived in a small fishbowl.

As an adult, Cindy loves to tell this story by her friend Mary Clare Carlson about goldfish and fishbowls:

> The size of a goldfish depends on the size of the place where it lives. If you keep a goldfish in a small fishbowl, it stays small: only 2 inches long. But

institution (in stuh **too** shuhn): a place where groups of children and adults with disabilities sometimes live

if you place the goldfish in a large pond, it grows much larger, up to 13 inches long.

People are a lot like goldfish. If we live and work in a small and limited area, our lives stay small, and we do not mature and grow as adults. If we live and work in many different and challenging places in the community, spending time with many different people, our lives grow large, and we mature as adults. We can do more than anyone ever dreamed we could do.

Choose the pond, not the fishbowl!

When Cindy was 26 years old, she finally moved into a house with other people in a neighborhood. For the first time in her life, she began to feel that the fishbowl was

A recent picture of Cindy.

2

getting larger. When she moved into her own apartment 3 years later, she was out of the fishbowl at last.

No one ever imagined that once Cindy was on her own, she would have dinner at the White House twice with 2 different American presidents, travel around the world, and give a speech in front of 15,000 people. But she did!

This is Cindy's story—and how she chose the pond instead of the fishbowl.

2

Nobody Loved Her

Cindy Bentley's first day of life in Milwaukee, Wisconsin, on October 18, 1957, was almost her last. Her doctors thought she might not live more than 24 hours. Why? While Cindy's mother was pregnant, she used illegal drugs and drank a lot of alcohol. Cindy didn't die, but her mother's drug and alcohol use did leave Cindy with an **intellectual disability**.

Having a disability means that someone can't do something or has difficulty doing something that a person without a disability can do. If the disability is permanent, it will last a person's whole life. Cindy has a permanent intellectual disability.

intellectual disability (in tuh **lek** choo uhl dis uh **bil** uh tee): a disability related to thinking and reasoning

What Are Disabilities?

There are many kinds of disabilities. People with physical disabilities have trouble using part of their body. They may not be able to walk or use their arms. People with **sensory** disabilities have trouble seeing or hearing. People with **behavioral** disabilities have trouble controlling their actions. People of any age can have a disability. Some disabilities are permanent, and some are **temporary**. Some can be helped with medications and others with special equipment such as a wheelchair.

Some people find learning easier than other people do. People with intellectual disabilities are slower to learn and may have more difficulty understanding new ideas or information than people without intellectual disabilities. They may have trouble learning to talk, to read, or to do other things that their friends can easily do. In the United States, as many as 3 million people have an intellectual disability.

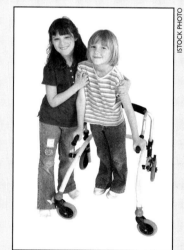

This young girl with a physical disability uses a walker.

sensory: related to the senses   behavioral (bi **hay** vyur uhl): related to how one acts or behaves
temporary: lasting only a short time

After Cindy was born, her father left her mother. Cindy never met him. Her mother went to prison for taking drugs. Cindy saw her mother only twice during her entire life. Cindy lived in many different **foster homes** during her childhood. She had a terrible experience in one of them. Her foster mother was so angry with her that she lit Cindy's shirt on fire. Cindy suffered **third-degree burns** on her stomach, back, and right arm. Once again, Cindy's doctors thought she might not survive. But she did. She spent 6 months in the hospital receiving treatment for her burns. She had 9 surgeries to repair the damage. It was very painful.

When Cindy left the hospital, she was placed in one foster home after another. She was an unhappy child. Her mother had left her. She'd had bad experiences in foster homes. She felt that nobody loved her.

foster home: a home where adults are paid by the state to care for children unable to live in their own homes
third-degree burn: a serious burn that damages all the layers of the skin

Why Does Someone Have a Disability?

There are many different reasons why someone can have a disability. Sometimes the cause of the disability is known. Often it is not. Sometimes the cause happens before a baby is born. The baby could have a disease that is passed from parent to child that causes a disability. The baby's mother may have been ill or exposed to something during her pregnancy that harmed the baby developing inside her. Sometimes the cause happens after a baby is born, as with an accident or an illness.

COURTESY OF SPECIAL OLYMPICS WISCONSIN

Cindy's mother drank alcohol when she was pregnant with Cindy. Sometimes if a pregnant woman drinks alcohol, her baby is born with **fetal alcohol syndrome** (FAS). FAS affects each baby differently. It can cause the baby's brain, heart, and other organs to develop incorrectly. A person born with FAS can have intellectual, physical, and behavioral problems. Cindy's disability could have been prevented if her mother had not used alcohol and illegal drugs during her pregnancy.

*This young boy has a developmental disability. He is excited because he got a **strike**.*

fetal (**fee** tul) **alcohol syndrome** (**sin** drohm): a set of physical, behavioral, and intellectual disabilities in babies born to mothers who drink alcohol during pregnancy   **strike**: knocking down all ten pins in bowling

3

An Unhappy Childhood

When she was 8 years old, Cindy's **social workers** decided that she should live in an institution. The institution Cindy was sent to is now called the Southern Wisconsin Center for the **Developmentally Disabled**. Southern Center is located in Union Grove, south of Milwaukee.

COURTESY OF GREG WILSON

Southern Center a few years after it was built.

social (**soh** shul) **worker**: a person whose job it is to help people in need
developmentally (di vel uhp **men** tuh lee) **disabled**: having a mental and/or physical disability that begins in childhood and usually lasts throughout life

At Southern Center, Cindy spent most of her days and nights in a large room with about 40 girls and 2 staff workers. The staff would wake the girls each morning. They'd take the girls to the bathroom 5 or 6 at a time. There were no doors or walls between toilets. Then the staff placed the girls on a long, flat table and washed them.

Next, the girls ate breakfast. The food was served on trays with different sections like the ones used in school cafeterias. Cindy thought all the food was awful. The oatmeal was the worst! She had to eat it every day.

After breakfast, the beds were pushed against the walls, and the girls had nothing to do until the next meal. There were no activities, books, or games. Some of the girls attended school in a different building. Occasionally, some went into the community on field trips. Most of the time, though, they just stayed in the room. Lights were turned off by 7:30 p.m. The girls had to go to sleep whether they were tired or not. Like all of the children who lived there, Cindy had no toys, no place of her own, and no privacy.

Cindy cried a lot. No one understood why she was crying. Maybe she cried because she was afraid. Perhaps she cried because she felt so lonely. Sometimes she didn't even know why she was crying. When she did cry, the staff yelled at her and told her to stop. That made her cry even more.

Cindy lived in a room like this at Southern Center—with 39 roommates!

Cindy remembers feeling so sad that she'd stand in a corner bumping her head against the wall. She thought everyone hated her. So she was mean to other people before they could be mean to her. She had temper tantrums. She sometimes became so angry that she hit and kicked the staff. Once, she even threw a chair through the window!

Why was Cindy so angry? She hated living at Southern Center. She wasn't allowed to decide anything for herself. She couldn't make any choices at all. The staff made all the decisions about what Cindy could wear and what she could eat. They decided when she went to bed and when she got up in the morning. Sometimes Cindy had to earn **tokens** for good behavior so that she could watch TV, buy candy, or even go to school. Can you imagine having to earn the right to watch TV? What would it feel like to have no toys or no place of your own? Wouldn't this make you angry?

When Cindy's behavior was especially bad, she was sent to live in a different building where the children with the worst behavior problems lived. Cindy now shared a room with 3 other girls. Once, in the middle of the night, one of girls bit her for no reason. When Cindy tried to defend herself, she was told that *she* was the problem because she had misbehaved so much.

token: a small object, such as a ticket or fake coin, that can be used in place of money

11

Cindy didn't have a mother or father who would listen to and protect her. She didn't have friends to stick up for her. She felt as though she was all alone in the world. She didn't trust adults or kids. She knew bad things had happened to her and would continue to happen to her, so why care about anything? She felt hopeless.

Institutions for People with Developmental Disabilities

If you were a child with an intellectual disability and lived in Wisconsin in 1896, you probably lived at home with your family. In 1897, things changed. The State of Wisconsin built its first institution for people with intellectual disabilities. Families were encouraged by doctors to **put away** their child with a disability and try to forget that the child had ever been born. As soon as this institution opened, 215 people were sent to live there. Many stayed there for the rest of their lives.

In 1919, Wisconsin opened a second institution for 86 **residents** in Union Grove, Wisconsin. Many years later it became known as the Southern Wisconsin Center for the Developmentally Disabled. When Cindy Bentley was sent there to live in 1966, the Center had more than 1,300 residents. With so many people living together,

put away: to send someone away to an institution   **resident**: person who lives in an institution or nursing home

12

no one received **individual** attention. The staff at the institution decided what the residents ate, when they went to bed, and what clothes they wore.

The workers who built Southern Wisconsin Center.

By the 1980s, many people in Wisconsin no longer believed that a person who had a disability should be sent to live in an institution. They didn't think it was a good idea for people with disabilities to live apart from their families and the rest of their community. Instead, they believed that people with disabilities—just like people without disabilities—should be able to go to school in their neighborhoods, visit friends, shop for their own clothes, have a job, and do all the things people without disabilities can do.

New laws were passed to help people move from the institutions to homes in their communities. The new laws helped people move out of institutions. Now, fewer and fewer people live at Southern Wisconsin Center. Many people with disabilities and their friends hope that someday all the institutions for people with disabilities will be closed. They hope that all people with disabilities will be able to live in communities with their family and friends.

individual: single or separate

13

4

A First Friend

Sometimes, Cindy was sent from Southern Center to live in foster homes. She hated this. She thought her foster parents were mean. Although she often was unhappy at Southern Center, she wanted to return there because it was at least familiar. It was as close to "home" as she knew. So, Cindy would misbehave in the foster homes or run away so that the foster parents would send her back to Southern Center.

Cindy bakes cookies with other Southern Center students.

At first, Cindy attended school inside of Southern Center. She didn't like school. She felt her teachers didn't like her. Her teachers were **frustrated** because

frustrated (frus **tray** tid)

14

Cindy didn't try hard and didn't work up to her **potential**. She often misbehaved.

In fifth grade, Cindy started going to a school outside Southern Center in Racine, Wisconsin. Many of the other students were mean to Cindy. They called her hurtful names. Cindy hated being teased.

Sticks and Stones May Break My Bones, but Names Can Also Hurt Me

Have you ever been called a name that you did not like? People with disabilities are often called hurtful names. *Idiot, stupid,* and *dummy* are all words that are used to **insult** people who are slower learners. The word *retard* is especially hurtful. Using these words about people with disabilities is no different from using a word that is hateful to describe people who are different from you because of their race, religion, or sex.

The words we use are important. Words change the way we think about a person. Saying someone is **confined** to a wheelchair is very different from saying that person is using a wheelchair. If we say that someone *uses* a wheelchair, we see the wheelchair as something the person controls to move around. If we say the

potential (puh **ten** shuhl): what you are capable of achieving   insult: to make fun of or put down
confined: unable to leave

15

person is *confined* to a wheelchair, we see that person as stuck or unable to move. These are 2 very different pictures of the same person.

This book uses *people first* language. People first language means instead of referring to someone by a disease or disability (such as "a disabled person"), we say a "person with" a disease or disability. This language tells what the person *has,* not what the person *is.* People first language was developed by people with disabilities who said, "We are not our disabilities. The disability is only a small part of who we are—we are people first."

This young girl uses a wheelchair to get around.

Cindy's worst school experience happened a few years later in her high school gym class. The girls were learning how to swim. When the other girls saw the burn scars on Cindy's arms, they said, "We don't want no burn person in this water." Cindy answered, "Take it or leave it. I'm getting in the water. You can pass or you can flunk." Cindy had decided to stand up for herself.

When she was younger, Cindy had nearly drowned in Lake Michigan. As a result, she was terrified of water. Although Cindy hated swimming, she was determined to pass all of the swim tests. She passed every test until it was time for the final test: **treading water**. Only half of the girls in the class passed the test. Cindy made sure she was the last person to take the test. She was so afraid that she was shaking. But she passed. Cindy was learning that trying hard and standing up for herself felt good.

Little by little, good experiences—such as passing the swimming test—began to change how Cindy thought about herself. Three experiences in particular had a **profound** effect on Cindy's life. When she was 10, Cindy went to church services at Southern Center. She began to develop faith in God. She began to believe that not everything that happens is bad. She began to trust that God would help her to survive.

treading water: swimming in place with the body in a straight up-and-down position   **profound**: very deeply felt

She became less angry. Her faith in God made her believe that she never was alone or without help.

Cindy is standing to the right behind the athlete getting ready to compete.

Around the same time, Cindy began to **compete** in Special Olympics. Special Olympics holds athletic **competitions** for people who have intellectual disabilities. In 1970, when she was 12 years old, Cindy competed in the second **International** Special Olympics Summer Games in Chicago. Much to her surprise, she took first place and won gold medals in 2 short running races: the 50-yard dash and the 100-yard dash. Cindy began to look at herself differently. She began to think of herself as "an athlete."

Cindy receives a gold medal for running at a Special Olympics event.

compete (com **peet**): to try to do better than others in a task, race, or contest   **competition** (com pe **ti** shun)
international: involving different countries

18

What Is Special Olympics?

Special Olympics is an international program of sports training and competition for people with intellectual disabilities. The idea for Special Olympics came from **Eunice** Kennedy Shriver, the sister of **former** president John F. Kennedy. One of their sisters, Rosemary, had an intellectual disability. She lived in an institution in Wisconsin most of her life. Eunice Kennedy Shriver wanted every child to have the **benefit** and fun of competing in sports. So, in June 1962, she invited 35 boys and girls with intellectual disabilities to Camp Shriver, a **day camp** at her home in Rockville, Maryland.

COURTESY OF SPECIAL OLYMPICS, INC.

Children at Camp Shriver in 1962.

In 1968, Eunice Kennedy Shriver organized the first Special Olympics World Summer Games in Chicago, Illinois. Nearly 1,000 athletes attended! They competed in 3 events: **track and field,**

Eunice (yoo nis)   **former**: from before or earlier   **benefit**: something that is good for you
day camp: camp where kids go for the day but don't stay overnight   **track and field**: a group of sports events that includes running, jumping, and throwing contests such as hurdles, pole vault, and shot put

swimming, and floor hockey. Slowly but surely, Special Olympics has spread around the world. In 2008, more than 2.5 million people from 165 countries competed in 30 sports at Special Olympics World Games. Eunice Kennedy Shriver died in 2009, but her **legacy** is not forgotten. Her son, Tim Shriver, is now in charge of Special Olympics.

Eunice Kennedy Shriver and a Special Olympics athlete.

The third life-changing experience for Cindy happened when she was 22 and still living at Southern Center. Chris Ziegler was hired to work as a **recreational therapist** at Southern Center. Chris liked Cindy immediately. They were about the same age, and they both liked sports. Chris became Cindy's running coach, helping her train for track and field. Their friendship built slowly. Cindy would be friendly for a while. Then she would do or say something that made her feel bad about herself. When that happened, she would

legacy: something handed down from one generation to the next   **recreational** (rek ree **ay** shu nuhl) **therapist**: someone who helps people who have a health problem or disability by using sports, art, music, dance, games, and other activities

become **negative**. She refused to do anything Chris suggested. Chris remained positive even when Cindy threw temper tantrums. She joked with Cindy and continued to encourage her. Chris never gave up on Cindy and always showed Cindy that she cared about her.

Like Cindy, Chris loved to run. She ran around Southern Center during her lunch breaks. When Chris saw Cindy run, she told Cindy that she could become a good runner and might enjoy running with her. Cindy didn't believe her. Chris was

COURTESY OF GREG WILSON

running at least a mile. Chris told Cindy she could do it, too. Chris said they would start running shorter distances before they built up to longer distances.

Cindy began running with Chris. She often whined and complained.

Cindy's love of running started at Southern Center.

negative: always saying no

But she continued running. Chris refused to listen to Cindy when she said, "I can't do it." Over time, Cindy came to trust Chris. Cindy began to feel better about herself. She began to develop **confidence** because of Chris's encouragement and from knowing that she *could* run long distances. For the first time in her life, she trusted another person. She learned she had people who cared about her. She found that she didn't want to disappoint them.

Cindy had finally found something she enjoyed doing and was good at: sports. She began to participate in every Special Olympics sport played at

Cindy, top row, third from right, with her Southern Center softball team after winning Special Olympics ribbons.

Southern Center: bowling, basketball, softball, and track and field.

confidence: strong belief in oneself or one's abilities

PHOTO BY JAN FITZGERALD

Cindy waits for softball practice to begin.

Cindy changed. She became a happier person. She smiled and laughed more often. She discovered that she enjoyed competing. She changed from being someone who didn't care about succeeding in anything to someone who wanted to be great at everything.

Cindy also became a more caring person. She began to help some of the other athletes at Southern Center who were training for Special Olympics. She taught them how to run faster and how to throw a ball. She had never before been willing to help anybody. Now, helping others made her feel good. Having a friend whom she could trust made all the difference in the world to Cindy.

5

On Her Own

In 1984, when Cindy was 26 years old, she moved out of Southern Center. She was afraid she wouldn't make new friends. Chris and other staff members told Cindy that she was ready to move on. After living in an institution on and off for 18 years, she finally would live in the community. Cindy now says, "That's when my life began."

Cindy moved into a **group home** in Milwaukee. At the group home she lived with 5 other adults who also had disabilities. They were all **supervised** by a **counselor**. It was scary for Cindy to move to a place where she had to learn so many new things and had to make so many decisions. At Southern Center, everything had been done for her. Someone woke her up, cooked her food, and told her what to do. Now she had to learn skills such as how to set an alarm clock and how to cross the street safely.

group home: a place where 3 or more adults live who need help caring for themselves   **supervised:** watched over or directed   **counselor** (**kouns** ler): someone who gives advice or helps with problems

Cindy even had to learn how to shop. The first time she went shopping for clothes, she was **overwhelmed** by all the choices. She worried about things such as, "What kind of material should I choose? What if I pick the wrong size?" There were too many choices, so Cindy didn't buy anything. Cindy was also given a **legal guardian**, Jan Fitzgerald, to help her learn how to live in the world outside of Southern Center. At first, Cindy called Jan 3 or 4 times a day to ask questions and talk about her worries. Jan said, "Cindy did not know how to handle this great big world." Cindy felt lost and lonely.

Cindy was 26 when she moved out of Southern Center.

Cindy rides a **toboggan** for the first time with her friend, Tammy Backey.

overwhelmed: to feel as though there is too much going on at once   **legal guardian**: a person chosen by a court of law to make decisions for another person, often because the person has a disability or serious illness
toboggan (tuh **bah** gin): a long, flat sled with a front edge that turns up

25

Slowly, Cindy began to feel more comfortable living in Milwaukee. She liked living in the group home better than living at Southern Center. But she didn't like living with 5 other people.

Cindy gets help with her bank account from **mentor** Caryn Bub.

She wanted to be on her own. In 1987, Cindy moved into an apartment with only one roommate.

Cindy and her roommate did not get along. Her roommate left after a few months. Cindy now lived alone. But she worried that

Cindy in 1988, at home in her very own apartment.

her neighborhood wasn't safe. She'd forget to pay her bills. She didn't understand how to **budget** her money. Living by herself was difficult for Cindy.

mentor: a trusted teacher or adviser   **budget**: to make a plan for how money will be earned and spent

A friend of Cindy's helped her find an apartment in a safer neighborhood. People were hired to help her live on her own. They helped her pay the bills on time and budget her money. At times, Cindy felt lonely. She didn't know what to do about it. One time she was so lonely that she pretended to be sick and was taken to the hospital. A friend was so worried about Cindy that she rushed to the hospital. Her friend became very angry when she learned that Cindy had pretended to be sick. She told Cindy that there were better ways to get attention.

Cindy never pretended to be sick again. But she still didn't know what to do when she felt lonely. Jan solved this problem by giving Cindy a cat. Cindy named the cat Tory. She immediately loved this sweet kitty. Tory liked to climb on bookcases. Sometimes he couldn't get down, and he'd whine during the night. Cindy didn't mind. Now, whenever she was home, she had company. Cindy was learning how to take care of herself and her pet cat.

Living on her own, Cindy could now choose how to spend her time for the first time in her life. She knew that she wanted to work, just as other adults did. While living at

PHOTO BY JAN FITZGERALD

Cindy relaxes with her first cat, Tory.

the group home, she had worked putting nuts and bolts into packages and putting labels on magazines. But Cindy wanted to do more interesting work than that.

A few months after moving into her own apartment, Cindy got a new job working for a Milwaukee organization that helped people with disabilities. Her job was to **recruit** volunteer speakers. Cindy had to find speakers to teach skills to people who have disabilities. These skills included learning things like how to prevent fires from occurring in homes. Cindy was excited by this opportunity to do work she enjoyed.

One year later, Cindy found another job taking care of children while their parents exercised at the gym. Cindy loved

recruit (ri **kroot**): to get a person to join a group or organization

28

the children and had fun in this job. Cindy was learning that she had many skills. She learned that she was able to work at many different kinds of jobs.

When the child-care job ended, Cindy thought, "I'm not gonna feel sorry for myself." Instead, she volunteered at a **nursing home**. Cindy read to the residents, brought them water, and played bingo with them. After several months, she was offered a job helping the activities director. Cindy now was paid for doing many of the same things she'd been doing as a volunteer. Cindy loved this job. She worked at the nursing home for nearly 3 years.

Cindy gets ready for work.

When a friend told Cindy about a job opening at McDonald's, Cindy applied. She served coffee, cleaned tables, and swept the floors. At first, Cindy was very happy with this job. "I liked working at McDonald's. They treated me like a regular **employee**,

nursing home: a residence for adults who need 24-hour care   **employee** (em **ploi** yee): someone who works for a person or company

not like a person with a disability." Many of the McDonald's customers knew Cindy by name. They looked forward to seeing her because she was so friendly. Some even hired Cindy to babysit for their children.

When Cindy worked at McDonald's, several customers knew her by name.

Eventually, though, Cindy became bored with this job and was ready to do something else. She wondered if she'd ever find a job she wanted to stay at for a long time.

In 1998, the Marshall Field's department store held a **bake sale** to raise money for Special Olympics. Cindy helped with the sale. At first, she sat at a table with other volunteers and watched the customers walk past without buying anything. Cindy then started introducing herself to the customers as they walked into the store. She encouraged them to buy a cookie or a brownie to help Special Olympics. Soon, all of the baked goods were sold.

bake sale: a sale where homemade cakes and pies are sold to raise money for a cause

A Marshall Field's employee had been watching Cindy that entire day. Before Cindy left for the afternoon, she was offered a chance to have a **job interview**. She soon was hired to work in the **stockroom**. To get to work on time, Cindy had to get up at 3:30 a.m. She dressed, ate breakfast, and then had to take 3 different buses to get to her job by 5:30 a.m. Cindy was proud to be able to get up so early to go to work. She also was proud that she had learned how to take the buses. "I don't know how I did it, but I did it. It was real hard," she later remembered.

Living on her own also meant that Cindy had the freedom to choose what to do when she wasn't working. What choices did she make? Like most people, Cindy spent time with friends and went out to places she enjoyed. Cindy also wanted to help other people. She had enjoyed her

Cindy cheers for the Milwaukee Brewers baseball team.

job interview: a meeting to talk about getting a particular job   **stockroom**: the room in a store where goods are kept until they go on the shelves

work volunteering at the nursing home, so she began to look for other places to volunteer.

One of Cindy's first volunteer jobs was to give out food at a **food pantry**. Cindy explained, "I like to give back to my community. I don't believe in sitting in my apartment. You can't find out about people and help people unless you're out there."

At one of her volunteer jobs, Cindy helps wrap gifts.

At another volunteer job, Cindy helped mothers who had been on drugs or in jail. They were in a program to learn how to be better parents. Cindy helped with cooking, passed out food, and played games with the children. She volunteered because she didn't want any of the children to have to grow up the way she had. Cindy thought if somebody had been there to help her mom, perhaps she wouldn't have had such a hard childhood.

food pantry: a service that provides food for people who are homeless or very poor

6

Female Athlete of the Year

After leaving Southern Center, Cindy wanted to keep competing in Special Olympics. When she moved to Milwaukee, she called the Milwaukee Special Olympics office. With the help of Karin Hawley, the staff person, Cindy soon found a new Special Olympics group to join.

PHOTOT BY SUE NEUPERT

Cindy poses with her Special Olympics basketball team after winning gold.

bocce (bah chee): lawn bowling

Which sports did Cindy play? She played as many sports as she could. In summer, she competed in tennis, soccer, volleyball, **bocce**, and track and field. In winter, she competed in basketball, bowling, speed skating, and snowshoeing. Cindy especially enjoyed team sports, such as **doubles** tennis, because she liked working with teammates. She said, "You have to remember that everybody is the star of the team. There's no 'I' in team."

Cindy with teammates Lynn Turner and Lucy Swietlik at a track meet.

PHOTO BY SUE NEUPERT

Competing in Special Olympics also opened the door to a new opportunity: public speaking. When Cindy joined Special Olympics in Milwaukee, Karin Hawley was often asked to speak to organizations who wanted to **contribute** to Special Olympics. When Karin gave a speech, she often asked Cindy to go with her. Cindy spoke at these events, too. She was especially good at sharing why Special Olympics was so important to her. Although Karin found Cindy to be very

doubles: a game played with partners, 2 against 2   **contribute** (kuhn **tri** byoot): to help an organization by giving money or volunteering

helpful, the main reason she invited Cindy was because she liked to be with her so much. Like Chris Ziegler, Karin had become Cindy's good friend.

How Does Special Olympics Work?

Special Olympics athletes can train in as many sports as they choose. Athletes have to be at least 8 years old and have an intellectual disability. They must train for 8 weeks in a sport before they can compete. In competition, athletes are divided into groups based on their age and skill level.

Athletes compete at the local, state, and national levels. Athletes who take first place in these competitions can choose to take part in a **lottery**. The athletes whose names are chosen in the lottery can compete in Special Olympics World Games. Special Olympics World Games takes place in a different country every 2 years.

A Special Olympics Wisconsin team carries their banner with the Special Olympics **Oath**.

lottery: a way of choosing someone to win or to be part of something just by chance, for example, drawing a name out of a hat **oath**: a serious promise

In 1988, Special Olympics began the "Athletes for **Outreach**" program. The program trained athletes with disabilities to make **presentations**. The idea was for Special Olympics athletes to share what made Special Olympics special, and why others should join. Karin asked Cindy if she'd like to be in the first Wisconsin training session. Cindy jumped at this opportunity. She volunteered because she trusted Karin and because it sounded interesting. At the training session, Cindy learned about the **mission** of Special Olympics and how to give speeches. Soon, she used what she had learned in her own speeches.

The team USA-Wisconsin snowshoe members display their gold medals.

A U.S. postage stamp honoring Special Olympics.

outreach: the act of telling other people about a program or service   **presentation**: a speech in which information is introduced to teach or convince an audience   **mission**: the meaning or purpose of an organization or cause

When Cindy began to speak in public about her life and Special Olympics, amazing things started to happen. The people who listened were often moved to tears. They were **inspired** by what she had to say. Cindy told her story about nearly dying the day she was born. She talked about her mother being in prison and how it felt to grow up without any family support

"In Special Olympics it is not the strongest body or the most dazzling mind that counts. It is the invincible spirit which overcomes all handicaps. For without this spirit winning medals is empty but with it there is no defeat."
Eunice Kennedy Shriver

COURTESY OF SPECIAL OLYMPICS WISCONSIN

Cindy is at the center of this poster that tells people the message of Special Olympics.

or love. She spoke about her unhappy life in foster homes and Southern Center. And then she shared how her life really began once she left Southern Center. She described her rich and happy life living on her own, and her love of sports and Special Olympics. Cindy said she loved sports and Special Olympics so much that she promised herself, "I am going to compete until I die."

inspired: encouraged

37

At first, Cindy didn't want to talk about her past. But when she saw that people admired her for surviving so many difficulties, she became more confident. When she spoke about herself as a child, she would often say, "I was not a nice person. I was pretty mean." But it was clear she'd fought many battles and had never given up. People who listened to her speeches felt that they, too, could **overcome** difficulties in their lives. They saw that Cindy wasn't bitter about the past. They saw how positive she was about her life and her future.

Speaking in public **before** large groups of people was an especially brave thing for Cindy to do. When she was younger, she had received **speech therapy** because her speech was **slurred**. Sometimes she wondered if people who heard her could understand her words clearly when she spoke. Now she was speaking in public in front of hundreds of people!

Cindy gives a speech with Dennis Alldridge, President of Special Olympics Wisconsin.

overcome: to deal with or get past a problem or challenge   **before**: in front of   **speech therapy**: help for people with speech and language problems   **slurred**: unclear, because sounds run into one another

Cindy started making speeches for Special Olympics in 1988. Three years later, her contributions to Special Olympics were recognized around the country. In 1991, when she was 34 years old, Cindy was chosen to be the Special Olympics International Female Athlete of the Year. She was chosen because of her athletic performance, **character**, leadership, and work in the community. She was now a role model for athletes across America.

COURTESY OF CINDY BENTLEY

Cindy Bentley, Special Olympics International Female Athlete of the Year.

Cindy began to speak at Special Olympics conferences around the United States. She had 2 particularly scary experiences in her travels. One was speaking before a crowd of 1,000 people. Cindy

character (**kair** ik tur): what sort of person you are

39

had never spoken in front of so many people. She was really scared, but she forced herself to tell the story of her life.

Equally scary for Cindy was riding an escalator. When Cindy was a child, her foot got caught in an escalator. She was hurt, and she never forgot this experience. After that, she was afraid of escalators. She would always ride an elevator or take the stairs to avoid riding on an escalator.

One time in Washington, D.C., however, there was no elevator or stairs, and Cindy had to ride an escalator to get to a conference where she was going to speak. She had no choice. Cindy was terrified. But she knew she had to do it, and so she did. Cindy was very proud of herself for facing her fear. When she was asked, "What was scarier, speaking before 1,000 people or riding the escalator?" she answered, "Both!"

An escalator like the one that scared Cindy.

7

"We're Not Kids. We're Athletes!"

Special Olympics helped people with intellectual disabilities to become athletes. Yet, they had never asked the athletes themselves for ways to make the organization better. This changed in 1993, when Cindy was chosen along with a few other athletes to share their thoughts with the staff who worked at Special Olympics.

Cindy waits with other Special Olympics athletes to talk with officials.

The discussion was led by a popular TV talk show host. By this time, Cindy was not afraid to speak to anyone. When it was her turn to speak, she asked, "Why didn't you ask us sooner what we thought about Special Olympics?"

That wasn't the only thing that bothered her. When the talk show host called Cindy and her fellow athletes "kids," Cindy felt insulted. She corrected him saying, "We're not kids. We're athletes!"

Cindy with members of the Wisconsin Team who went to the 1995 Special Olympics World Summer Games.

Two years later, in 1995, Cindy was chosen to compete in her second Special Olympics World Summer Games in New Haven, Connecticut. This time, she would compete with athletes from all over the world. When she learned she had been selected, she was so excited that she screamed. She was proud that she was going to represent Wisconsin and the United States. Twenty-five years earlier, Cindy had won gold medals in track and field at the World Games in Chicago. This time she

A ticket for the opening ceremonies to the 1995 World Summer Games.

was competing in tennis. At the games in New Haven, Cindy won a silver medal in **singles** tennis and sixth place in women's doubles. Cindy loved competing again in the Special Olympics World Games.

Earning the medals was especially satisfying for Cindy because she hadn't been playing tennis very long. Tennis took a lot of **coordination**, which did not come easily to her. The stiffness in her arm from the burns she had received as a child

Cindy and her tennis **opponent** at the 1995 World Summer Games.

made it even more difficult. She improved by hitting the ball again and again. Why did Cindy take up a sport that was so difficult for her? "I like to try challenging things," she says proudly. "I don't like to take things that are too easy."

Cindy received another great **honor** at the 1995 World Summer Games. She was chosen to carry the Wisconsin banner and lead the

singles: a game played one-on-one   **coordination** (koh or duh **nay** shuhn)   **honor**: praise or recognition
opponent (uh **poh** nuhnt): someone who is against you in a fight or contest

76 members of the Wisconsin team into the stadium during the **opening ceremony**. As she entered the Olympic stadium, a video of her story was shared on a jumbo-sized screen for everyone in the stadium to see. In the video, Cindy said that she wanted to be a great winner in life and that it was most important to her to have "the simple things of love, happiness, caring, and to be free."

At the opening ceremony, people held up cards to show what country the athletes entering the stadium were from.

As Cindy led the athletes into the stadium, it was clear that she had become something no one thought was possible: a leader. For years, she had been changing the way people

opening ceremony (ser uh moh nee): the celebration that marks the start of the Special Olympics, with a parade of athletes from each country or state

thought about people with disabilities. People saw that she had a disability, but they soon paid *more* attention to her abilities and what she *could* do. Cindy made it easy for people who had never met anyone with a disability to get to know her. She became a bridge builder between people with disabilities and people without them.

In 1996, Cindy was given another chance to be a leader. Wisconsin's governor at the time, Tommy Thompson, asked her to serve on the Wisconsin Council on Developmental Disabilities. This organization works to improve the lives of people with disabilities. Cindy was one of the first people with an intellectual disability chosen to be on the council. Cindy's job would be to help the other members of the council understand the needs of people like her, who have an intellectual disability.

In 1999, Special Olympics Wisconsin decided to ask an athlete to be on its **board of directors**. This person would help make decisions for the state's 10,000 Special Olympics athletes. Cindy became the first athlete to serve on the board. She was chosen for many reasons. She was one of the first

board of directors: a group of people chosen to make decisions for an organization or company

athletes to take on many of the different Special Olympics roles: volunteering at Special Olympics events, recruiting volunteers, raising money, speaking to the public about Special Olympics, and competing as an athlete. And Cindy already had a lot of experience participating in meetings with the

Wisconsin Council on Developmental Disabilities.

Cindy also was chosen because she was very good at convincing new athletes to join Special Olympics. She would speak

FRONT

BACK

The front and the back of a Special Olympic gold medal.

almost anywhere—in the grocery store, in the shopping mall, or in her neighborhood—to young people and their parents about how Special Olympics changed her life. Cindy may have recruited more athletes to join Special Olympics than anyone else in Wisconsin.

8

Speaking for 2.5 Million Athletes

Cindy's successful work on the Special Olympics Wisconsin board soon brought her another opportunity to be a leader. In 2000, Special Olympics International—the organization that was in charge of Special Olympics for every country around the world—chose Cindy to be a Global Messenger. For 2 years, Global Messengers travel throughout the world telling people about Special Olympics. Cindy was one of 12 athletes chosen to **represent** more than 2.5 million athletes! The other Global Messengers came from China, Bosnia, Botswana, Canada, Jordan, Greece, Venezuela, and the United States.

Cindy took her duties as Global Messenger seriously—especially making speeches.

represent: to stand or act for

In May 2000, the Global Messengers traveled to the Special Olympics European Games in **Groningen**, Netherlands. At the opening ceremony for the games, Tim Shriver spoke. He is the head of Special Olympics and the son of its founder, Eunice Kennedy Shriver. Suddenly, Tim asked Cindy to give a speech. He felt confident that Cindy could come up with the right words to thank all of the people who had volunteered to help Special Olympics. She did indeed.

Cindy traveled to many countries as a Global Messenger. In 2001, she was chosen to light the Special Olympics torch as it began the 5,500-mile journey from

Cindy with athletes in the Netherlands. Tim Shriver, head of Special Olympics, is in the middle with a black shirt.

Greece to Alaska for the Special Olympics World Winter Games. In Greece, Cindy had many amazing experiences. She met the **prime minister** of Greece and other important world leaders.

Groningen (**groh** ning uhn)   prime minister: the head of a government

48

During her visit to Greece, Cindy got to visit temples thousands of years old.

The Mayor of Athens awards medals to the Global Messengers.

On one Greek island, Cindy tasted a new food. She was sitting with a Global Messenger from Canada. They were about to choose a snack, when he said, "You don't come all the way to Greece not to eat something different." Cindy was willing to have new experiences, and so she took a bite—octopus! Not all new experiences are good experiences. When Cindy tasted the octopus, she said, "It was disgusting. Yuck!"

Cindy with her friend and escort, **Jeanne Hrovat,** in Alaska.

Two days after she returned home from Greece, Cindy boarded an airplane to **Anchorage**, Alaska, for the World Winter Games. She went to Alaska with her good friend and Special Olympics **escort**, Jeanne Hrovat. While they were there, Jeanne had a day when she was feeling very sad and she began to cry.

Cindy comforted her friend. Jeanne later said, "As Cindy's escort, my role was to take care of her needs, but in this case I was the one who needed care. Cindy reached out to me, and I felt the warmth of her heart. In that moment, I understood we were equal partners and true friends."

Jeanne Hrovat (jeen **roh** vat)   **Anchorage** (an kor **idj**)   **escort**: a person without a disability who accompanies a Special Olympics athlete to a competition

50

As a Global Messenger, Cindy was often interviewed by reporters.

Cindy's experiences as a Global Messenger changed her in many ways. She learned how to handle herself in many different situations. In everything she did, she tried to be a good role model for athletes around the world.

A Special Olympics International staff person, Kirsten Suto Seckler, said that many people have mistaken ideas about people with intellectual disabilities. They think that people with disabilities can't do things on their own. But Cindy shows us that isn't true. Here's what Kirsten said

51

about Cindy: "Cindy has **defied** all of the **stereotypes** in her life. She lives **independently**. She holds jobs. She travels the world. She's met presidents of the United States. She's won gold medals, and she's gone to the World Games. She's never let anyone tell her, 'No you can't.' I think there's something special about Cindy, and we don't want it to just stay in Wisconsin. We want the whole world to experience that."

defied: refused to obey; challenged   **stereotype**: an overly simple idea or opinion of a person, group, or thing
independently: on one's own

9
Cindy's Dream Job

When Cindy became a Global Messenger in 2000, she also began a new job. In 1999, Cindy had helped create a new organization, People First Wisconsin. The members of People First Wisconsin, like Cindy, had disabilities. The purpose of the organization was to fight for the **rights** of people with disabilities. Cindy's new job had 2 responsibilities. The first was to help people with

Cindy at her desk in the People First Wisconsin office.

rights: something that the law says you can have or do, such as the right to vote or the right to go to school

Cindy decorated the wall behind her desk with posters and photographs.

disabilities learn how to speak for themselves. The second was to help the public understand the rights and strengths of people with disabilities.

Working for People First Wisconsin was Cindy's dream job. She explained, "I wanted to help people with disabilities across the state and get them the services they deserve. We need **affordable housing** and health care, and I will fight as long as it takes to make this happen."

affordable (uh **for** duh buhl) **housing**: places to live that people with low incomes can afford to rent or buy

Nothing about Me Without Me

"Nothing about me without me" is a saying that is very important to people with disabilities. In the past, many people with disabilities were treated as though they were young children. Important decisions that affected their lives were made by people without disabilities. People First Wisconsin is an **advocacy** organization created to help people with disabilities learn to speak up and make decisions for themselves. The

People First Wisconsin

See our d̶i̶s̶Ability

COURTESY OF PEOPLE FIRST WISCONSIN

organization is called "People First" because they want people to remember that they are *people* first, and their *disability* is second.

This was Cindy's first job working in an office. She had a lot to learn. Unlike her other jobs where she was told what to do, this job required her to figure out what needed to be done. One of her jobs was to make phone calls to set up meetings. At first, she was easily frustrated. When she called people, sometimes they wouldn't return her call. She felt that "I called them, they didn't call me back, so that's that." Cindy

advocacy (**ad** vuh kuh see): support for an idea or a plan

needed a lot of encouragement not to give up when people didn't return her messages. Fortunately, she received help from other people who worked in her office. She also had a **job coach** who helped her with her tasks.

There were many other parts of the job that were hard for Cindy. Sometimes she had to argue with people who would get angry at her. One thing she fought for was closing the state centers for people with disabilities. That included the Southern Center where she had spent so many years of her life. She wanted the people who still lived in the state centers to be able to live in the community.

PHOTO BY CAROLINE HOFFMAN

Cindy speaks at the Wisconsin State Capitol to ask lawmakers to close state institutions like Southern Center.

Some of the people who attended those meetings were against closing the state centers. They believed that people with **severe** disabilities needed to

job coach: a person who is paid to help someone with a disability at his or her workplace   severe (suh vir): serious

be protected by living in institutions. Some of the people arguing were people Cindy had known when she lived at Southern Center. They used to tell Cindy what to do. Now, Cindy could say what she wanted to say.

She argued that Southern Center was not a good place for people with disabilities to live. Speaking against the Southern Center was scary for Cindy. Yet she did it anyway. She was willing to fight because she thought it was important to let all people with disabilities have more rights and live in the community.

Civil Rights for People with Disabilities

Civil rights are the rights of all citizens in a country to be treated equally and fairly. Many laws have been passed in the United States to make sure that everyone has the same civil rights. In 1920, women gained the right to vote. In the 1960s, the Civil Rights Acts were passed to make sure that African Americans had equal rights under the law. But people with disabilities didn't have laws to protect their rights until about 30 years later.

The United States **Congress** passed the Americans with Disabilities Act in 1990. This law made it illegal to **discriminate** against people with disabilities at work, at school, and in other public places. For example, a movie theater must make changes so that all people, including those who use wheelchairs, can get into the theater. Bus lifts, **accessible** bathrooms, and **sign language interpreters** are all examples of changes that can be made that help people with disabilities to participate in the same kind of activities as people without disabilities.

A group of people with disabilities and their supporters gathered at the state capitol in Madison to ask lawmakers to provide more money for their cause.

President George Bush signs the American with Disabilities Act on July 26, 1990.

Congress (**kong** gris): the part of our government where laws are made   **discriminate** (dis **krim** uh nayt): to treat some people better or worse than others without any fair reason   **accessible** (ak **ses** uh buhl): able to be entered or used by a person who has a disability   **sign language interpreter**: a person who translates the spoken word into American Sign Language for people who are deaf

58

Over time, Cindy became very good at speaking for herself and others. She's spoken to doctors, teachers, police officers, and many others to help them understand how to work with people with disabilities and treat them with respect.

Cindy also helps other people with disabilities speak out for themselves. She explains how she was afraid to speak up for herself, how she found the strength to do it, and how important it is for them to speak up, too. She inspires many people who have disabilities. They see Cindy as someone who looks like them, talks like them, and has had experiences like them. After hearing her speak, many feel that they can stand up for their rights, too. Cindy says, "I help people with disabilities to believe in themselves."

Cindy received this award for her work helping people with disabilities.

10

Cindy Gives Away Her Gold Medals

Even when she was busy with Special Olympics and working, Cindy found time to volunteer. She especially liked helping mothers who had used drugs or were in prison. Over time, 3 of those mothers died. One of the staff from Shade Tree Family Resource Center also died. These people had been important to Cindy, and she wanted to remember them. Cindy decided to place one of her gold medals inside each of their **caskets**. Cindy explained, "I gave the medals because I thought they were heroes. I just changed it from a Special Olympics medal to a bravery medal." Another volunteer said of Cindy, "That's one of the most touching things I've ever seen. She is an amazing woman."

Cindy gave away medals that looked just like these.

casket: a long wooden or metal container into which a dead person is placed for burial

It was particularly generous of Cindy to give away her medals. As an adult, she finally had things of her own. At Southern Center, she couldn't own *anything*. Now she was giving away her most precious possessions.

But Cindy was just getting started in sharing her gold medals. She heard about a 10-year-old girl named Christina who slipped while was climbing a tree in her backyard. Christina grabbed a power line as she fell and was badly burned. Christina was taken to the same hospital Cindy had been sent to as a child after she was burned. When Christina would not take part in the **therapy** the hospital staff wanted her to do, Cindy was asked to speak with her.

When Cindy arrived at the hospital and was about to enter Christina's room, she heard Christina arguing with her mother. Christina did not want to do the exercises that would help her recover her abilities. Cindy walked into the room and asked to speak with Christina alone.

Cindy told Christina that she, too, had been burned as a child. She showed Christina the scars from her badly burned

therapy: a treatment for an illness, injury, or disability

arm. Cindy told her that her burned arm is the arm she now uses to play tennis. She explained how important it was for Christina to do her exercises so that *her* arm wouldn't stiffen up. Cindy gave Christina one of her gold medals for being a brave little girl. She told her to look at the medal to help her remain brave when things got hard or painful, or when she felt sad.

By the time Cindy left, Christina promised that she would do her exercises as long as the doctors wanted her to do them. Christina's mother said her daughter's changed attitude happened because "Cindy worked her magic."

Over the years, Cindy has given away many of her "bravery" medals. She especially likes to tell the story of one particular gold medal she gave away—to a United States president. In her lifetime Cindy has met 2 U.S. presidents, President Bill Clinton and President George W. Bush.

On December 14, 2000, President Bill Clinton and First Lady Hillary Rodham Clinton hosted a concert at the White House called "A Very Special Christmas from Washington, D.C."

Many famous musicians and movie stars were invited to the concert to celebrate the spirit of Special Olympics. Cindy and other Global Messengers were invited, too. The concert took place under a huge tent on the White House lawn. When Cindy learned that she would be going to dinner at the White House, she wanted to look her best. She bought a new necklace, earrings, shoes, and a fancy evening dress.

Cindy with the Global Messengers in front of a Christmas tree at the White House.

At the dinner before the concert, Cindy sat at a table with Hillary Clinton and her daughter, Chelsea. Chelsea was then 20 years old. What do you talk about with the president's daughter? Pets! Cindy asked Chelsea how her dog Buddy and her cat Socks got along. Chelsea answered that they didn't get along at all. The 2 pets always had to be separated. Cindy told Chelsea about her cat, Baby. Among the many presents Cindy received that day from the White House was a book written by Hillary Clinton called *Dear Socks, Dear Buddy: Kids' Letters to the First Pets.*

After the White House dinner, Cindy, the Global Messengers, President Bill Clinton and First Lady Hillary Rodham Clinton enjoyed a special concert with singer Darlene Love.

One year later, Cindy returned to the White House with 5 other Global Messengers to celebrate the Special Olympics. This time they were the guests of President George W. Bush and First Lady Laura Bush. The dinner took place only 3 months after the **September 11, 2001**, terrorist attacks on the

September 11, 2001: the day that became known as 9/11, when Islamic terrorists flew airplanes into the World Trade Center in New York City and the Pentagon in Virginia

United States. Everything was carefully planned. After dinner, 3 Global Messengers would speak and then a famous **blues** musician, B. B. King, would perform.

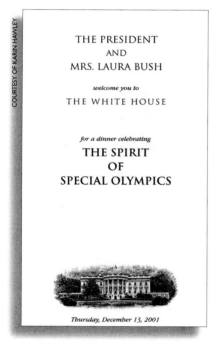

THE PRESIDENT
AND
MRS. LAURA BUSH

welcome you to
THE WHITE HOUSE

for a dinner celebrating
THE SPIRIT
OF
SPECIAL OLYMPICS

Thursday, December 13, 2001

This is the invitation Cindy received for dinner at the White House with President George W. Bush and First Lady Laura Bush.

Before dinner, Cindy spoke with Tim Shriver. She showed him a Special Olympics gold medal she had brought from Wisconsin to give to President Bush. She asked Tim if he would give it to the president. Tim was so moved by Cindy's kindness that he told her that she should give it to the president herself. He received permission from the White House for Cindy to give the president the medal.

When it was time for Cindy to speak, she walked up to President Bush and said, "My team won a gold medal last week in volleyball, and we decided to give the medal to you, Mr. President, because you have kept us safe." President

blues: a type of music, often expressing sadness, first sung and played by African Americans

Bush leaned down, Cindy put the medal around his neck, and he kissed her left cheek.

Cindy will never forget that the president kissed her cheek. She'll also never forget what the president wore on his feet. When President Bush bent down to receive Cindy's medal, she noticed he was wearing cowboy boots. Stitched on the boots were the words, "President of the United States."

President George W. Bush shows his boots with the presidential seal.

Cindy reaches out to shake hands with President George W. Bush after presenting him with one of her gold medals.

11

Choose the Pond, Not the Fishbowl!

Cindy has created a rich life for herself. She lives each moment of each day to its fullest. She's had a lot of help along the way. She's received help in part because she's been willing to ask for it.

Cindy goes to the library regularly. Whenever she feels sad, she rereads her favorite book, *Charlotte's Web*, by E. B. White. In this story, Wilbur didn't believe in himself because he was a pig. Charlotte the spider risked her life to save Wilbur. When Charlotte died, Wilbur took care of her babies. The book reminds Cindy to believe in herself and in her friends.

Cindy has learned many things from playing sports. She's learned how to **discipline** herself to become better at things. She's learned to feel good about herself, particularly when she is helping a teammate. She believes she has become

discipline (**dis** uh plin): to control your actions through training

a stronger person, both in sports and outside of sports, too. Cindy's newest sport is snowshoeing. In snowshoeing, as in other areas of her life, Cindy has learned how to pick herself up when she falls—again and again.

Cindy also has learned that she likes people and people

like her, too. As a child, she had no friends. She didn't trust anyone. Now she has many, many friends. Of the many speeches Cindy has given, her

Cindy gets ready to compete in the Special Olympics State Winter snowshoeing race.

most **memorable** one occurred in 2007. She was asked if she would thank the Lions Club International for supporting Special Olympics. The Lions Club is an international volunteer organization that works to help prevent blindness and reaches out to communities in need. Cindy was eager to speak. She

memorable (**mem** ur uh buhl): easily remembered or worth remembering

was excited because the Lions Club would be presenting her good friend, Special Olympics chairman Tim Shriver, with an award.

Cindy Bentley, spirit of a champion!

When Cindy arrived in Chicago, she was surprised to learn she would be presenting her speech to 15,000 people! The thought of speaking before so many people made Cindy very nervous, but she was determined to speak anyway.

The president of the Lions Club introduced Tim Shriver and gave him the Lions' Club **Humanitarian** Award for his work with Special Olympics. Cindy was asked to sit on the stage. While Tim spoke, Cindy started getting so nervous that she began crying. Cindy explained what happened next:

humanitarian (hyoo man uh **tair** ee uhn): having to do with helping people and relieving suffering

I asked God to give me the strength to get up and give my speech to the Lions' Club International, which deserved the thank-you because of their kindness. I knew that I needed to do this speech and it could not come from Tim Shriver. It had to come from an athlete.

Cindy speaks at the Lion's Club International in front of 15,000 people.

I got up, Tim Shriver introduced me, and I asked God to give me the strength to give me the right words and to do the best that I could. I stood up straight and gave myself the confidence to do my best for the whole

Cindy claps as Tim Shriver receives an award from Lions Club International President Jimmy Ross.

Special Olympics **movement**. I felt it was my duty as a Special Olympics athlete and a Global Messenger and a role model to other athletes, and because I

movement: a group of people who have joined together to support a cause

70

took the oath of the Global Messenger, that I would do the best that I could do. Also, I remembered all my mentors and Mrs. Shriver telling the athletes that we have the potential to do whatever we put our minds to do.

When I got up there and looked out at all the people out there, my stomach hurt. But I knew I had to give the speech. So I did the speech and received a **standing ovation**.

Cindy still faces many challenges because of her disabilities, but she focuses on her abilities instead. She has a poster on the wall of

Cindy has come a long way!

standing ovation: enthusiastic recognition, usually with loud applause and standing

her apartment that reminds her, "You can't change your past, but you can change your future."

It's been many years since Cindy left Southern Center to live out in the world on her own. That small fishbowl of her childhood is long gone. Since she's been living in the community, she's grown, and grown, and grown! Cindy has taught many people why it is so important to be able to choose the pond instead of the fishbowl.

Appendix

Cindy's Time Line

1957 — Cynthia Bentley is born in Milwaukee, Wisconsin.

1966 — Cindy is placed in Southern Wisconsin Center in Union Grove, Wisconsin.

1970 — Cindy wins 2 gold medals in the second International Special Olympics Summer Games in Chicago, Illinois.

1984 — Cindy moves out of Southern Center and into a group home in Milwaukee, Wisconsin.

1987 — Cindy moves into her own apartment in Milwaukee.

1988 — Special Olympics Wisconsin chooses Cindy to be part of the first group of Athletes for Outreach.

1991 — Cindy is chosen as Special Olympics International Female Athlete of the Year.

1995 — Cindy competes in the Special Olympics World Summer Games in Connecticut. She wins a silver medal in singles tennis and takes sixth place in women's doubles tennis.

1996 — Governor Tommy Thompson chooses Cindy to serve on the Wisconsin Council on Developmental Disabilities.

1999 — Cindy helps start People First Wisconsin.

Cindy is the first athlete chosen to serve on the board of directors of Special Olympics Wisconsin.

2000 — Special Olympics International names Cindy as a Global Messenger.

Cindy attends "A Very Special Christmas from Washington, D.C." with the Clintons at the White House.

2001 — Cindy attends her second "A Very Special Christmas from Washington, D.C." at the White House and gives a gold medal to President George W. Bush.

2007 — Cindy speaks at the Lions Club International convention in Chicago, Illinois.

2010 — Cindy competes in the Special Olympics Summer Games in Omaha, Nebraska.

Glossary

Pronunciation Key

a	c<u>a</u>t (kat), pl<u>ai</u>d (plad), h<u>a</u>lf (haf)	**oh**	<u>o</u>pen (**oh** puhn), s<u>ew</u> (soh)
ah	f<u>a</u>ther (**fah** THur), h<u>ea</u>rt (hahrt)	**oi**	b<u>oi</u>l (boil), b<u>oy</u> (boi)
air	c<u>a</u>rry (**kair** ee), b<u>ear</u> (bair), wh<u>ere</u> (whair)	**oo**	p<u>oo</u>l (pool), m<u>o</u>ve (moov), sh<u>oe</u> (shoo)
aw	<u>a</u>ll (awl), l<u>aw</u> (law), b<u>ough</u>t (bawt)	**or**	<u>or</u>der (**or** dur), m<u>ore</u> (mor)
ay	s<u>ay</u> (say), br<u>ea</u>k (brayk), v<u>ei</u>n (vayn)	**ou**	h<u>ou</u>se (hous), n<u>ow</u> (nou)
e	b<u>e</u>t (bet), s<u>ay</u>s (sez), d<u>ea</u>f (def)	**u**	g<u>oo</u>d (gud), sh<u>ou</u>ld (shud)
ee	b<u>ee</u> (bee), t<u>ea</u>m (teem), f<u>ea</u>r (feer)	**uh**	c<u>u</u>p (kuhp), fl<u>oo</u>d (fluhd), b<u>utto</u>n (**buht** uhn)
i	b<u>i</u>t (bit), w<u>o</u>men (**wim** uhn), b<u>ui</u>ld (bild)	**ur**	b<u>ur</u>n (burn), p<u>ear</u>l (purl), b<u>ir</u>d (burd)
ɪ	<u>i</u>ce (ɪs), l<u>ie</u> (lɪ), sk<u>y</u> (skɪ)	**yoo**	<u>u</u>se (yooz), f<u>ew</u> (fyoo), v<u>iew</u> (vyoo)
o	h<u>o</u>t (hot), w<u>a</u>tch (wotch)	**hw**	<u>wh</u>at (hwuht), <u>wh</u>en (hwen)
		TH	<u>th</u>at (THat), brea<u>the</u> (breeTH)
		zh	mea<u>s</u>ure (**mezh** ur), gara<u>ge</u> (guh **razh**)

accessible (ak **ses** uh buhl): able to be entered or used by a person who has a disability

advocacy (**ad** vuh kuh see): support for an idea or a plan

affordable (uh **for** duh buhl) **housing**: places to live that people with low incomes can afford to rent or buy

bake sale: a sale where homemade cakes and pies are sold to raise money for a cause

before: in front of

behavioral (bi **hay** vyur uhl): related to how one acts or behaves

benefit: something that is good for you

blues: a type of music, often expressing sadness, first sung and played by African Americans

board of directors: a group of people chosen to make decisions for an organization or company

bocce (**bah** chee): lawn bowling

budget: to make a plan for how money will be earned and spent

casket: a long wooden or metal container into which a dead person is placed for burial

character (**kair** ik tur): what sort of person you are

civil rights: the rights of all citizens in a country to be treated equally and fairly

compete: to try to do better than others in a task, race, or contest

Congress (**kong** gris): the part of our government where laws are made

confidence: strong belief in oneself or one's abilities

confined: unable to leave

contribute (kuhn **tri** byoot): to help an organization by giving money or volunteering

counselor (**kouns** ler): someone who gives advice or helps with problems

day camp: camp where kids go for the day but don't stay overnight

defied: refused to obey; challenged

developmentally (di vel uhp **men** tuh lee) **disabled**: having a mental and/or physical disability that begins in childhood and usually lasts throughout life

discipline (**dis** uh plin): to control your actions through training

discriminate (dis **krim** uh nayt): to treat some people better or worse than others without any fair reason

doubles: a game played with partners, 2 against 2

employee: (em **ploi** yee): someone who works for a person or company

escort: a person without a disability who accompanies a Special Olympics athlete to a competition

fetal (**fee** tuhl) **alcohol syndrome** (**sin** drohm): a set of physical, behavioral, and intellectual disabilities in babies born to mothers who drink alcohol during pregnancy

food pantry: a service that provides food for people who are homeless or very poor

former: from before or earlier

foster home: a home where adults are paid by the state to care for children unable to live in their own homes

group home: a place where 3 or more adults live who need help caring for themselves

honor: praise or recognition

humanitarian (hyoo man uh **tair** ee uhn): having to do with helping people and relieving suffering

independently: on one's own

individual: single or separate

inspired: encouraged

institution (in stuh **too** shuhn): a place where groups of children and adults with disabilities sometimes live

insult: to make fun of or put down

intellectual disability (in tuh **lek** choo uhl dis uh **bil** uh tee): a disability related to thinking and reasoning

international: involving different countries

job coach: a person who is paid to help someone with a disability at his or her workplace

job interview: a meeting to talk about getting a particular job

legacy: something handed down from one generation to the next

legal guardian: a person chosen by a court of law to make decisions for another person, often because the person has a disability or serious illness

lottery: a way of choosing someone to win or to be part of something just by chance, for example, drawing a name out of a hat

memorable (**mem** ur uh buhl): easily remembered or worth remembering

mentor: a trusted teacher or adviser

mission: the meaning or purpose of an organization or cause

movement: a group of people who have joined together to support a cause

negative: always saying no

nursing home: a residence for adults who need 24-hour care

oath: a serious promise

opening ceremony (**ser** uh moh nee): the celebration that marks the start of the Special Olympics, with a parade of athletes from each country or state

opponent (uh **poh** nuhnt): someone who is against you in a fight or contest

outreach: the act of telling other people about a program or service

overcome: to deal with or get past a problem or challenge

overwhelmed: to feel as though there is too much going on at once

potential (puh **ten** shuhl): what you are capable of achieving

presentation: a speech in which information is introduced to teach or convince an audience

prime minister: the head of a government

profound: very deeply felt

put away: to send someone away to an institution

recreational (rek ree **ay** shu nuhl) **therapist**: someone who helps people who have a health problem or disability by using sports, art, music, dance, games, and other activities

recruit (ri **kroot**): to get a person to join a group or organization

represent: to stand or act for

resident: person who lives in an institution or nursing home

right: something that the law says you can have or do, such as the right to vote or the right to go to school

sensory: related to the senses

September 11, 2001: the day that became known as 9/11, when Islamic terrorists flew airplanes into the World Trade Center in New York City and the Pentagon in Virginia

severe (suh **vir**): serious

sign language interpreter: a person who translates the spoken word into American Sign Language for people who are deaf

singles: a game played one-on-one

slurred: unclear, because sounds run into one another

social (**soh** shul) **worker**: a person whose job it is to help people in need

speech therapy: help for people with speech and language problems

standing ovation: enthusiastic recognition, usually with loud applause and standing

stereotype: an overly simple idea or opinion of a person, group, or thing

stockroom: the room in a store where goods are kept until they go on the shelves

strike: knocking down all 10 pins in bowling

supervised: watched over

temporary: lasting only a short time

therapy: a treatment for an illness, injury, or disability

third-degree burn: a serious burn that damages all the layers of the skin

toboggan (tuh **bah** gin): a long, flat sled with a front edge that turns up

token: a small object, such as a ticket or fake coin, that can be used in place of money

track and field: a group of sports events that includes running, jumping, and throwing contests such as hurdles, pole vault, and shot put

treading water: swimming in place with the body in a straight up-and-down position

Reading Group Guide and Activities

Discussion Questions

- Cindy has said, "You don't have to have a happy childhood to be a happy adult." How did she turn her unhappy childhood into a happy adult life? Name 3 obstacles that she had to overcome, and how she overcame them.

- When Cindy was in her swim class, other students made fun of her. What did she do that helped her with her anger? If you hear someone make fun of another person, what can you do? How can you stop one person from bullying another or making fun of another?

- Learning she is not alone has been an important part of Cindy's journey. Name 2 people from the book who were important to Cindy. Why were they important to her? Now, think of ways she has been a friend to others. How did having a friend help Cindy be a friend?

Activities

- Read about different groups who have fought for their civil rights (women, African Americans, people with disabilities) and write a short essay about how they won their struggle to get equal rights.

- Cindy has become well-known because of her ability to speak about Special Olympics and the rights of people with disabilities.

Why was speaking so important to her? What steps did she take to overcome her nervousness? Think about something you care about. Write a list of reasons you believe in your cause. Then create a speech to present to your class to pursuade them it is important.

Cindy has spent a lot of time volunteering—at a food pantry, at a nursing home shelters, and for the Special Olympics. In what ways did volunteering help her? How did volunteering help the groups she worked for? Brainstorm something you and your class or a group of friends can volunteer to help with. How do you think this activity might help you as well as the organization you're volunteering to help?

To Learn More about Disabilities

Dinn, Sheila. *Hearts of Gold: A Celebration of Special Olympics and Its Heroes*. Farmington Hills, MI: Blackbirch Press, 1996.

Kennedy, Mike. *Special Olympics*. Danbury, CT: Children's Press, 2003.

Kent, Deborah. *Athletes with Disabilities*. London: Franklin Watts, 2003.

————. *The Disability Rights Movement (Cornerstones of Freedom)*. Danbury, CT: Children's Press, 1996.

———— and Kathryn A. Quinlan. *Extraordinary People with Disabilities*. Danbury, CT, Children's Press, 1997.

Sabin, Ellen. *The Special Needs Acceptance Book: Being a Friend to Someone with Special Needs*. New York: Watering Can Press, 2007.

Acknowledgments

It has been our privilege and delight to have our friend Cindy Bentley share her life story with us. Thank you, Cindy, for your generosity with your time, your kindness, your willingness to answer questions even about the hard parts of your life, and just for being you.

We are grateful to Jennifer Ondrejka and the Wisconsin Board for People with Developmental Disabilities for their willingness to provide the funds to make this book a reality.

Learning more about Cindy through interviews with her many friends, coaches, and colleagues has been an inspiring journey. Our favorite interview question to ask was, "What acts of kindness did Cindy perform?" The answer was consistently, "Do you have all day to hear about them?" These stories significantly increased our understanding and appreciation for Cindy and the rich life that she has created.

Thanks to all of you who shared your stories and/or photos, including: Gerry Born, Sandra Butts, Mary Clare Carlson, Ruthann Cherne, Judy Fell, Jan Fitzgerald, Chris Glader, Karin Hawley, Jeanne Hrovat, Kelly Kloepping, Mary Mackey, Howard Mandeville, Lisa Mills, Nancy Molitor, Sue Neupert, Jennifer Ondrejka, Laura Owens, Tom Pezzi, Kirsten Suto Seckler, John Shaw, Kevin Szydel, and Greg Wilson.

Judy Landsman, Jennifer Ondrejka, and Deborah Waxman edited early drafts of Cindy's story and made innumerable helpful suggestions. Sara Phillips of the Wisconsin Historical Society Press helped shape Cindy's story into a book we believe does justice to Cindy's amazing story. Bobbie Malone enthusiastically supported this endeavor and provided her inimitable assistance from start to finish.

85

Index

This index points you to the pages where you can read about persons, places, and ideas. If you do not find the word you are looking for, try to think of another word that means about the same thing.

When you see a page number in **bold** it means there is a picture on that page.